Table of Contents

Introduction

Chapter 1: The Intricacies of Latte Art

Chapter 2: A Lot of Ado Over Foam and Milk

Chapter 3: The Perfect Foam

Chapter 4: Pulling the Shots

Chapter 5: Free Pouring Technique

Chapter 6: Pouring the Heart Shape

Chapter 7: Pouring the Rosette Shape

Chapter 8: Pouring the Tulip Shape

Chapter 9: Pouring the Flower Shape

Chapter 10: Etching and Drawing Techniques

Conclusion

Introduction

Thank you for purchasing this book *"Latte Art: The Ultimate Barista's Guide To Stunning Coffee Art."*

The idea behind this book is to provide aspiring baristas with information, tips, and tricks that they can use to improve their latte art. The information contained in this book can also be used by non-baristas who just want to have great tasting and not to mention really delectable looking coffee in the morning – with or without an expensive espresso machine.

This book contains instructions on how to properly pull your espresso, make the perfect crema, pour latte art patterns, and etch artworks on foam. Examples have also been included so you can practice immediately even in the convenience of your very own kitchen.

May this book help you and inspire you to create tempting beverages that please the eye and delight the taste buds.

To your success,

Cheers!

Chapter 1: The Intricacies of Latte Art

For most of the English-speaking people of the world, the term "latte" will refer to that drink made with coffee and milk. Well, that is what the original term caffellatte actually means – coffee and milk. The term latte is actually shorthand for the original Italian term. If you visit Italy and order a "latte" there, don't be surprised if the locals serve you a glass of milk instead – well, latte is milk in Italian.

However you call it, whenever we say latte in this book we actually refer to a combination of espresso and milk. Well, enough of the geeky terminology. You will have to admit that making a good espresso is already a work of art in itself. However, we all know that a good latte is usually served with some form of creative artwork on top made from the milk that the coffee is served with.

You have to admit that the art on top of your espresso just makes the beverage yummier – well at least it looks more delish than ever. And this is where the term latte art comes into the picture. You can even say that there are a few people who obsess with the art on their cups more than the taste of their drink.

Latte art refers to the artsy patterns that are created on the foam that tops your espresso. It reflects the level of creativity of the barista who prepared your drink. To make these wonderful and eye-catching designs, the one preparing the drink should take extra care with the delicate foam floating atop that shot of espresso.

Anyone will admit that making consistent looking latte art will be pretty difficult. There are several factors that come into play here. These factors include the pour, the skill of the barista, and of course the quality of your espresso machine being used.

Origin and History of Latte Art

Even though lattes, the coffee plus milk combo drink, has been around since the 17th century, the art that you see on top of that shot of espresso is actually a modern invention. The actual craft of making art on your latte has grown independently from one country to the next with latte artisans hailing from different parts of the world.

However, they all share a common origin – the introduction of the espresso and the dawn of the microfoam. When the microfoam meets the crema then you can create that subtle surface that allows you to create patterns on top. This technique of serving coffee was created in Italy – presumably of course.

Latte art became a big hit in Seattle in the United States back in the '80s. The art of making images appear on top of your coffee was made popular by David Schomer. The secret behind good latte art is in the introduction of the microfoam, which Schomer says was the brain child of Jack Kelly back in 1986.

Skip three years into 1989 David Schomer took advantage of the possibilities that can be made with microfoam and created the heart pattern – which eventually became his brand's signature, the espresso vivace. Moving forward several years into 1992, Schomer introduced another pattern, the rosette or Rosetta, and yes people spell it in different ways.

Schomer also taught a class called "Caffe Latte Art" which is where he introduced the rosette pattern. The class of course taught students barista skills, specifically how to make latte art. Schomer also met with another familiar name in the modern coffee world – Luigi Lupi, and they eventually exchanged ideas about the subject of latte art.

The Science Behind the Art

If you think you can use the milk you bought from the grocery store straight from the can or the ones brought to you by the milk man,then think again. Believe it or not there is a bit of chemistry behind the process of making the perfect latte and latte art.

You need to mix two different colloids to make it all happen – the microfoam and your crema. First you need an emulsion which is made up of coffee solids mixed in water (thus making that familiar drink) and milk, which is already an emulsion from butterfat and water.

Note that all the colloids that go into your espresso with latte art on top will not last that long. They usually stay there for a few minutes. After a few more minutes they will begin to dissipate.

Every newbie barista should know that the two key ingredients for making really great latte is a fresh shot of espresso with a good amount of crema of course. The other half of the equation is steamed milk that is properly textured. These two are the foundations of your latte art. The milk needs to be denatured (we'll get into that in a minute) which is why you can't make latte art using regular milk straight out of the carton.

The Technique Behind the Art

Half of good latte art is really good latte. The other half is the skill (combined with experience) of the barista. Again, part of the skillset that you will need to acquire is the ability to make good espresso, with microfoam plus crema of course.

Before you can create any work of art, you're going to need a surface to work on. Your canvass in this case will be that creamy brown surface on top of the espresso. This surface is actually the emulsion called crema.

After the white foam from the milk is poured into the cup, it will mix in part with the brown or reddish colored espresso on the surface. This will create a creamy brown surface. A contrast will be created thus making the image form on top of your coffee.

Remember that you are using foamy milk. It has a tendency to rise to the top while the coffee liquid stays at the bottom. This separation of course won't last and the two will eventually mix together.

Moving the pitcher of milk around as one pours it into the cup will create a variety of designs. This is the method of making latte art that requires a good deal of skill and timing. You can't pour the milk too slow or else you lose the effect you want to achieve. Alternatively, instead of pouring the milk into the shot of espresso, you can create the milky surface and then etch your design using a stick. You can also use a stencil to create the patterns on top, which is somewhat easier.

Forms of Latte Art

There are basically two forms of latte art. The first one is called free pouring and the other one is called etching. Free pouring is more common in cafes in America although etching can be a lot easier – it can also require a lot of talent. Some artworks using etching may require 3 to 5 minutes but the creations can become truly stunning.

Free Pouring:

in free pouring, the barista pours the milk into the cup and creates images as the milk is poured in. The most common or should we say fundamental figures created using this method are the heart, rosetta, and the tulip. The rosette is also known as the fern since the rosette is a type of flowery fern.
Most of the time you will see the heart shape made on top of macchiatos. On the other hand, rosettes are usually made atop lattes, since they are more complex and require a lot more cup space.

In free pouring, a barista would either hold the cup at a level position or perhaps slightly tilted. After the foamy milk is poured into the cup, the foam will surface on one side as more milk enters the cup on the other. This effect is due to the tilt made.

The barista will then hold the cup at a level position to allow the rest of the foam to rise and as he or she is doing that he creates the designs by moving the milk pitcher around in predetermined motions. The pitcher can be moved from side to side or wiggled back and forth to create the desired effect.

The barista will then create a strike through pour starting from the top of the image created down to the bottom. This will part the pattern and split it into two. This strike through motion creates the center of the heart shape, the stem of the rosetta, and the center of the tulip. It basically bends the pattern to create the final outcome of the image that you want to make inside the cup.

A more direct pour will create a solid sort of rounded shape, which will become the heart shape later after you make the strike through motion. With a little variation in the motions, like a few wiggles that produce a larger stem and reduced lobe will create an apple like shape. It is recommended that beginners start by making the heart shape and then maybe experiment on the apple shape which allows them to get the hang of action of pouring milk.

The other patterns are more complex and will require more than a single pour of milk. The tulip for instance requires about three pours – one for the base, another for the middle, and the one last for the top of the tulip. We'll go over these shapes in the coming chapters.

Etching:

etched patterns and shapes are a lot simpler to make. You will still need to make the foam surface that serves as your canvass of sorts. The patterns you can make on the foam can be simple geometric patterns like stars, hearts, and such. You will be using cut outs that were made using templates.

The idea is to pour chocolate powder (or some other spice like cinnamon) top of the cut out so that an imprint will be made on the foam surface. You can then use a coffee stirrer to modify the pattern, add lines using chocolate, and incorporate other details.

Note that this method is relatively faster than pouring. That is why it is the easy choice for a lot of commercial chains. You can finish one cup in a minute or two and then serve it to your customer in waiting. Note that the patterns you make using the etching method will have a shorter life span compared to poured patterns. Etched patterns on foam tend to dissolve faster since you aren't pouring any additional milk into the cup.

In the next chapter we'll look into the process of making a perfect latte, which is one of the fundamental skill sets that any barista should have. Remember, that half of the job in making latte art is making delicious tasting latte. Your art won't be remembered if the coffee your customer drinks tastes awful.

Chapter 2: A Lot of Ado Over Foam and Milk

So, what's your fix? Is it the latte or is it the art on the latte? Or is it both? Whatever it is, one thing is for sure, if you're a coffee enthusiast you simply look up to a nice delectable warm cup in the morning (or whatever time it is you prefer to get a cup of coffee).

Making your shot of espresso a work of art is more than just an extra. Sometimes it is the thing that makes your day. You may have come across some sample of latte art that has brightened your day, right? Well, if you're interested in learning how to make your own latte art, then here it is. And it begins with the way you prepare the milk.

Not the coffee? Yes, not the coffee. But we'll get to that one later.

More Than Just Regular Milk

There was a guy who once asked if barista milk is better than any kind of milk for your latte. Dritan Alsela, social media sensation, barista, and coffee connoisseur, replied by just brushing the question aside with a wave of a hand. Why? Because there is no such thing as "barista milk." If someone tries to sell you one then you know that it's a sham.

Dritan once said that you can actually use any milk. Of course, not everyone agreed with him but he was happy to demonstrate that you can use any milk – that includes the milk your milkman delivered this morning.

Of course when we say "any milk" don't take it literally. You can use any type of milk except for the cold ones. Remember that it was mentioned earlier that there is a science behind the making of latte art.

You need steamed milk that has been properly textured. Remember that you are pouring microfoam into a cup of espresso. A barista will usually get steamed milk and then rapidly heat it. This heating of the milk and making the bubbles form in the milk jug is an important step. It is called denaturing. Denaturing alters the properties of the milk that you put into coffee.

So, how does denaturing work? Let's go back to the basics of milk to answer that question. What is milk made of? It has proteins, of course, it has fat, and it has sugar. What happens when it is super-heated really fast? That's why the milk is blasted with steam when you make latte.

Rapidly heating it breaks down the sugars and the fat within the milk making them smaller thus ending up as simple sugars. And that is why the milk gets sweeter. Ideally, you need to heat it up to 60 to 70 degrees Celsius or 158 degrees Fahrenheit. If the temperature goes up any higher then you essentially burn the milk and that will taste bad.

More Than Just Simply Pouring Milk

Now you know that you can't just take the milk inside the fridge and use it to make latte art. It has to undergo the denaturing process to create microfoam. Now, there are other things that you have to deal with when it comes to milk and microfoam.

Beginners also make the mistake of pouring milk too slowly. That's understandable of course. You're still figuring out how fast you should pour the milk so it is expected that there will be times when you will do that. Now, don't pour it too fast either – you don't want the foam to nose dive right to the very bottom of the cup.

Now, there is another reason why you shouldn't pour the milk too slowly. Pouring slowly will cause the milk inside the pitcher to separate to a certain degree. The result will be that the milk that goes into the cup gets less aerated. Guess where all the aerated milk goes to? If you said it stayed in the pitcher then you guessed correctly.

If the milk you pour into the beverage is less aerated or less frothy, then it will make life more difficult for you when you try to make latte art. Another effect of doing this is that the quality of the coffee is also affected degrading its taste and flavor.

Another classic mistake that people make is lifting the pitcher way too high when they make their designs. When you pour your milk to make a heart for example, you shouldn't raise your milk pitcher too high above the cup. When you do that, the milk dives deep into the cup, which practically ruins everything. Remember that the goal is to allow the milk to rest on top of the crema.

On the other hand, when you rest the spout of the milk just way too close to the cup, then you make another classic mistake. What happens when your spout is too close to the beverage? The milk you are pouring will tend to skim on the surface of your beverage. What happens is that no pattern is formed and you get frustrated. The idea is to raise the spout of the milk jug about 2 to 3 centimeters away from the beverage.

Now this will take some experimentation. Just remember that when you raise it too high the milk will start to skim the surface and you won't get the patterned effect that you were expecting. If that happens then lower the spout a little bit.

Now that you have a general understanding on how the milk is supposed to work when it comes to making latte art, it's time to move to the very first phase of making latte art; and that is to make the perfect foam. Remember that the quality of the foam you have will make or break your latte art.

Chapter 3: The Perfect Foam

The first phase to make some good latte art is to make some really good foam. Well, some would say to make the perfect foam – but you can't always do things perfectly, right? You have already learned about the details of milk and microfoam in the previous chapter. In this one, we will go over the details of actually making the microfoam for your latte.

Working with the Cold Milk

Now, this may sound confusing at first. Well, we did mention that we will superheat the milk really fast. I mean, the goal is to make the milk's temperature rise up to 60 to 70 degrees Celsius, right? Well, ideally, according to experience that is, just if you keep it somewhere between 60 to 65 degrees and everything will be just right. Trying to hit the 70 degree mark will be pushing it and you may end up burning the milk altogether.

So, how cold should your cold milk be? It's going to come from the fridge, right? Don't put your milk in the freezer – we want cold milk not frozen milk popsicles. A good temperature should be about 34°F or 1°C. That should do the trick.

You don't need to put the milk in the fridge overnight – just half an hour should be enough to get it down to that temperature. Notice that we are very particular about the temperature. It is crucial to the process, which is why you should invest in a good milk frothing thermometer.

Get one that is made out of stainless steel or at least the probe should be made of stainless steel. You can even order one from Amazon or eBay. You don't need to get one that is absolutely high tech. In fact, anything that costs less than 10 dollars will work just fine.

So, open your carton of milk and put the entire contents in your milk pitcher (and yes, you're going to need several pitchers). Place the pitcher of milk in the fridge and keep it there for 30 minutes. After half an hour check the milk's temperature. If it is anywhere around 34 degrees then take it out. The cold pitcher will also help you steam the milk much easier. A cold pitcher will help make the cream stiffer thus it will be a lot easier to handle. It will also help prevent any scalding.

You will have to transfer some of the milk to a separate jug. You only need a cup of cold milk in the jug that you will steam for your latte. Remember that you will steam this milk and create froth. The effect is that the milk will rise and increase in volume.

Steam Wand It Baby

The next step is to use your espresso machine's steam wand. Put it at the bottom of the pitcher. After that, turn on the steam. Now raise it until the steam wand is positioned near the top of the milk. Note that applying steam via the steam wand will make the milk rise, increasing its volume.

As the milk rises you need to lower the jug or else the wand will be caught in the middle of the milk's volume. Try to maintain the wand at about a centimetre into the milk from the top and not all the way into the bottom or middle of the milk.

One big no-no that you should avoid is making huge bubbles in your milk. If that happens then the milk has stretched. The effect you want to achieve is that velvety and smooth milk. That's the goal. Of course you're also going to get really foamy milk that rests on top of jug. You can't use that part coz it will just mess up your pour.

Now, once you notice that the volume has increased – it would appear now that you have two cups of milk inside the jug instead of just one, then the next step is to make the milk spin. Well, this may be an extra step for some but you should at least try it if you're just starting.

Turn up the heat and make the milk's temperature reach 100°F. Put your thermometer to good use. So, how do you make the milk spin? You do that by placing the steam wand deep inside the jug and position it close to the side. Angle it a bit so that the milk will spin in either a clockwise or a counter clockwise direction.

After giving the frothy milk a good spin, turn up the heat to 150°F. Now, here is the crucial part. One steamer will be quite different from another. Some will heat the milk really fast while others take a bit longer. Keep an eye on your thermometer. A good idea would be to just let the heat reach somewhere past 140 degrees and then remove the steam wand (well, it's more like pulling the jug away from the steam wand).

Some steamers heat the milk so fast that they have a tendency to burn the milk. Observe how your espresso machine's steamer works. What you want to achieve is some light bubbling as opposed to the formation of really huge bubbles. If you got that in the jug then what you have there is microfoam – nice foaming that doesn't compromise the consistency of the body of the milk.

Now, shut the steam. Push the wand back in place and give it a good blast to clear any milk that may be left inside. Wipe the wand clean with a wet cloth.

The Swirling and Pounding Action

You have seen this a lot of times, haven't you? Do you notice how baristas would pound their jugs on the counter as if they're killing a cockroach or some other insect? Well, they do that for a reason. They are actually making the milk swirl (well, they have removed the thermometer by then) by moving the milk jug around.

Swirling the milk around ensures that you get that much desired velvety texture. Of course, there will be a few big bubbles in there. So how do you deal with that? Pound the pitcher hard on the counter and then swirl it again a few more times. That should get rid of those huge bubbles.

The next step is to pour the top half of the contents of the milk jug into a different jug. This top half is usually thicker and frothier than the bottom half. You will work on the bottom half first, which is more velvety. When that is all used up, get the top half, swirl and bang it on the counter to reduce the thickness of the foam and then you can use it to make your latte art.

And there you have it. That's how you make the perfect foam – or something close to it.

What If I Don't Have an Espresso Machine?

Now, this is a good question – not everyone has a thousand-dollar espresso machine, right? Well, there are espresso machines that cost around 500 dollars apiece. An example of which is the Breville BES870XL, but that is still expensive. If you're really serious about your coffee and you want to really learn how to serve café level espresso complete with latte art then you should invest in one.

However, if you don't have the money for it yet, then what do you do? Well, you do it the old way. People used to steam milk without the need of a fancy, not to mention expensive, espresso machine.

So how do you do it the old-fashioned way? Here's how.

What you need:

- Sauce pan or pot (or any stainless-steel container/cooking appliance).
- Thermometer
- Milk jugs
- French Press

Here are the steps to do it:

1. Grab a sauce pan or some other stainless-steel container and place your milk in it. The container should be deep enough so your temperature probe can be dipped inside.
2. Heat your milk until it reaches 60 to 65 degrees Celsius or else you will end up burning your milk.
3. Once the milk reaches that temperature, take the milk out of the pot/pan and transfer it to a milk jug. Pour about a cup of the milk into a French press and cover it.
4. Pump the press to make the froth. Notice that doing so will make the milk rise.

5. Keep pumping until the milk has risen up to about a third of the way or double the original volume of the milk.
6. Transfer the frothy milk into another milk jug.
7. Give it a swirl and bang the jug on the counter to reduce the number of bubbles.

And there you have it. Now, believe it or not, the quality of the milk you make with this the old method is actually a lot better than using an espresso machine complete with steamer.

The milk you make with the old method is firmer and it lasts longer – which means your designs will remain on the coffee cup much longer (gives people more time to appreciate your work). The steamer on an espresso machine also has a certain disadvantage – it tends to heat up the milk way too fast. In fact, even though your thermometer may say that you have reached only up to 70 degrees Celsius, your steamer may already have burned some of the milk in the jug, which reduces the quality and taste of your latte.

Now, whichever steaming method you choose is all up to you. Espresso machine or not, the important thing is that your milk undergoes the denaturing process, which makes it delectable and naturally sweet.

Chapter 4: Pulling the Shots

Again, the following instructions assume that you have an espresso machine. Of course, if you don't have an espresso machine, then you can just prepare your coffee however which way you want to do it. Whether you have an espresso machine or not, you should still go over the info on this chapter so you at least know how to pull an espresso and maybe impress your friends while you're at it.

Start the Shots

As soon as you have foamed your milk, you should have started the shots. Some baristas even start the shots and then foam the milk while the espresso machine is working. Note that each shot of ground espresso you make should contain around 7 or 8 grams.

Now, your espresso machine will have a portafilter. You need to tamp down around 40 pounds of pressure on it. Some guys are too meticulous and would even try pushing down on a bathroom scale just to make sure they are using enough pressure. Now, you don't have to do that – well, you can do it if you really want to be precise.

Well, 30 to 40 pounds of pressure is about all the weight you can push down with just one arm – unless of course you are a power lifter then you can really push down a lot stronger than that. But for most adults, especially those of us who don't have the time to pump some really serious iron, then the single arm force should be enough.

Now, a burr grinder will also become a barista friendly tool. With it you can control how coarse or how fine the grind will be. Pull the espresso shots after that. You should pull the shots ideally within 21 up to 24 seconds. You will get that peculiar coffee flavour and it should have a bit of cream in the shot.

> **TIP:** So How Do You Tamp Properly?
>
> The following information will give you an idea about the basic technique required for properly tamping your coffee. The first step is to fill your portafilter so that the basket will be overflowing with coffee.

Take the lid, scrape all of the overflowing grounds of coffee. The outcome should be a slightly dipped patch of coffee in the container. Make sure to wipe off any loose grounds that have been left on the edges of the basket. This will ensure that there will be a snug fit later on before you apply hand pressure. Next, replace the lid on the doser and then you are ready to tamp the coffee grounds.

Raise the elbow of the arm that you will use to tamp the grounds with. Raise it up to about a 90-degree angle. With the hand tamp, holding the top, you will then pack the coffee grounds with a downward pressure – use the entire force of your arm as you do so.

If you do not apply that much force the coffee in the basket will be more of a loose pack. When the water pressure increases in the espresso machine later on, it will blast a hole amidst the coffee grounds, and the result of course is a brew that is of a far less quality than expected.

To prevent that from happening, use a downward motion twisting with your hand on the hand tamp. The goal is to create a level surface that will remain even – that means the coffee grounds have been packed in the basket very well. It will force the water later on to go through the coffee grounds rather evenly.

Now, we created some space earlier didn't we? That is a small bit of allowance so that the grounds can expand when the water passes through. The snug fit of the doser will prevent any damage that may occur to the gasket that can be found in the group head.

Before you begin extraction, make sure to purge the espresso machine first. Remember, purge before you insert the portafilter – that should be a rule of thumb. Purging will allow the machine to regulate the temperature a lot better. When you pull your shots, remember to judge by color. The output that you should get should look something like rust colored crema. This will ensure that it will last a long time.

Begin the extraction process with a drip first. After that, continue by extracting the more espresso ensuring that it comes out with a consistency similar to syrup.

Note that the espresso will tend to taste sweeter when you pull it close to 24 seconds. The amount of pressure you apply when you tamp down on the grinds will have a direct effect on the espresso shots and the length of extraction.

If you were able to tamp down while applying the appropriate amount of force then the espresso will extract evenly. That means the extraction process will be a bit slow. If you didn't tamp down well enough, which means you didn't exert the recommended amount of pressure then the espresso will tend to extract way too fast.

After the extraction, you can now pour your espresso shots into a mug where you can begin working your latte art. Of course, you will tend to make more espresso shots at certain times – let's say you made coffee for a small group of friends huddling inside your apartment.

Now, here is an important point: never let the espresso sit for more than 10 seconds before you add the steamed milk. When the shot sits for 10 seconds it is dead. You may have already heard this from baristas from Starbucks or from some other coffee place.

Remember, after pulling your shot, you have a 10 second window to pour your milk and then begin making your latte art. The shot is considered "dead" after 10 seconds. That doesn't mean the coffee is no longer drinkable. It simply means the quality of the espresso isn't as pronounced as it was originally intended.

Chapter 5: Free Pouring Technique

In this chapter we'll go over the steps used in the free pouring technique. There are a few things that you should mind whenever you pour the milk into the shot of espresso. You need to be mindful of the flow of your pour, the position of the cup and the milk jug, and the height of the jug in relation to the cup.

The first thing you need to do is to hold the cup at a slight angle. And then as you are about to pour the milk, make sure that the milk jug is at the same angle as the cup. The tip of the cup should be about parallel to the body of the jug. Make sure that there is a steady stream of milk as you pour from the jug to the cup.

The first step is to create that crema surface where you will make your latte art later on. Start pouring the milk a little high on the tilt that you made in the cup. Pour in a stead circular motion going around the perimeter of the cup. Keep pouring until the cup is already half full.

Remember that the height or distance of the jug from the cup is crucial at this point. The height of the jug from the cup should be at a distance of around 5 cm when you pour from the jug.

Remember that the speed of your pour and the angle of the jug in relation to the cup can make or break this part of your creation. Start by pouring slowly at first, which will help you get the proper momentum. After your initial slow pour, drop the jug to a level half the distance of the initial height of the milk jug. Note that if you pour too fast then the crema will break but if you pour too slowly then the microfoam, which is what you want inside the cup, will get left behind in the jug.

Remember to avoid wiggling the jug (like when you are nervous) when you pour the milk. You should move your pour from high up the angle of the cup to the lower end or bottom of the angled cup. Remember that you are trying to create a level surface. As one side of the crema rises it will create a rust-like color or stain. Notice that at the point when the jug's spout is closer to the cup, the crema will then start to rise.

How to Practice Without Wasting too Much Coffee or Milk

When you work your practice sessions you may end up with a hundred shots of espresso with different types of pours on it. Remember that you haven't even started making any images on the latte. What you want to master this time is the making of the crema surface, which should be nice and even.

Here's a way to practice so you get the hang of the process. You'll be needing the following:

- 1 empty cup
- Coffee grounds
- Your crema with perfect froth
- 2 jugs

Here's how you can practice:

1. Grab an empty cup.
2. Take a pinch of coffee grounds and put it in the cup.
3. Pour half of milk in the jug into a different jug and set that one aside.
4. Use the original jug that contained the milk. Bang it on counter a few times to remove any excess bubbles (i.e. large bubbles in the froth).
5. Practice your pour in circular motion to create the crema surface. Remember to keep the cup tilted at an angle the same with the jug as you pour. Both the cup and jug should be tilted at the same angle.
6. Pour until the cup is half full.
7. Drop the jug's level closer to the cup and make a solid pour at the center.
8. Notice that the crema will rise with some coffee stains in it and there will be a center that will not be as brownish as the rest of the crema surface.

If you are able to achieve that then you have done it really well. To practice again, pour all the contents of the cup back into the jug that you were using.

Repeat the steps again starting at step number 2.

Notice that after each round of pouring, you should be making a circular like center of the cup which is less brownish compared to the rest of the crema on the surface. If you have already used a lot of coffee then use the contents of the other jug (the one that contained the top half of the crema that you created).

Just make sure that the temperature of the milk is still within reasonable levels (that means it hasn't gotten too cold). Give the pitcher a few good bangs on the counter before you begin pouring.

Chapter 6: Pouring the Heart Shape

The heart shape pattern is the most basic pattern that every aspiring barista should learn. Remember, this was the very first design created in the world of latte art. Before you make this shape or pattern, you should do all the preliminary steps, which includes pulling and steaming your milk, pulling your espresso shot, and other steps which were discussed in the previous chapters.

Of course, for your practice sessions you can use the empty cup plus coffee grounds method. That way you don't waste espresso pulls and you don't make too much coffee that you will just throw away later on. Once you have gotten the hang of that, you should at then practice pouring on actual coffee. You can invite friends and family to taste your work in the process and ask them for a rather friendly critique.

Now, how do you pour the heart shape? Here's how:

1. After creating your crema surface, you should bring the jug closer to the cup.
2. Keep the cup at a level.
3. Begin pouring the milk in one area of the cup, actually near the top but close to the center (i.e. using your vantage point of course).
4. As you pour you should make a gentle side to side motion with the jug but maintain the position of the pour in the same place. This will make the design you are making to form a nice even circle at the center.
5. Keep going until you make a nice and big crema circle.
6. Move the jug slightly downward (i.e. closer to you) as you continue to pour and build the huge spot of crema in the middle.
7. Finish the pattern by making one final pour going from the top to the bottom of the pattern.
8. This will divide the pattern or design into two even sections or parts.
9. And voila! You have made your first latte art – the heart shape.

Be patient and expect to make mistakes during your first try. Use the empty cup practice method described in the previous chapter so you can have some allowance for failure. Do not try other pouring patterns until you master this one. The heart shape will be the basis of the other patterns or designs that you will pour when you create your latte art. Keep trying and don't give up.

Chapter 7: Pouring the Rosette Shape

Now we will go over the steps on how to make the rosette or rosetta pattern. As stated earlier, this design or shape was based out of the original heart shape. That means you will be doing pretty much the same steps but this time with only a few slight variations in the movements.

Here's how you make this pattern:

1. Now, let's assume that you are ready to pour milk into a shot of espresso. The first step as in the first pattern that was discussed in the previous chapter is to loosen the crema in the cup. That means that you will pour the milk from the jug around in circular motion.
2. Remember to move the jug around gently.
3. When the cup gets half full. This should be enough to allow you to pour more milk to create a rosette or rosetta pattern.
4. At that point you should see the crema lighten up. When it does that, it only means that the crema in the cup has begun to connect with the milk that you are still pouring in. when that happens you're supposed to start making your design.
5. Of course, it takes some practice before you can properly time when you're supposed to start. After some practice you'll get the hang of it and then you can wing it every single time.
6. Now, it's time to begin making the rosetta pattern. You can stop

pouring the base of the crema. Your cup should now be held at a level position.
7. Begin making your latte art by pouring near the top end of the cup (the side of the cup that is farthest from you using your very own POV).
8. When you pour make a steady wiggling action from left to right. This should be a faster wiggling action as compared to the one you did when you made the heart shape.
9. Make sure that the wiggling of the wrist that you are doing is consistent both in speed and in the range of motion.
10. Note that the range of the wiggling action that you make will influence the size of the leaves of the rosetta pattern you are making.
11. Try not to vary the distance of your wrist's swivel so that the leaves of the rosetta will not vary so much.
12. The speed at which you pour from left to right will determine just how many leaves will there be in the rosetta image. Try to go for as much as 7 or 8 leaves but it is all up to you. The more leaves you make the thinner they will be. If you swing slowly and make fewer leaves they will be fatter.
13. Move from the back end of the cup to its front end as you wriggle or swing your jug (well, more like zig-zagging). Make sure that you move in a steady and uniform manner as you go from one end to the other. If you vary the pace then the distance between the leaves will have a variance, which in part may ruin the symmetry of your creation.
14. You can pour a tiny heart pattern on the top if you wish. When you're done, raise the jug and then pour a straight line from the top of the rosette (where you placed your heart) to the bottom in one stroke or slash.
15. Notice the spaces in between the zigzags will become the leaves.

And that is how you make the rosetta. This pattern will be a bit more difficult compared to the heart shape and will require more practice. Take the time and you can also use the practice method described in an earlier chapter of this book to save latte shots.

Rosetta Making Tips

Here are a few tips to help you troubleshoot your movements in case you are having trouble making the rosetta.

- Make sure that the spout of the jug is as close to the surface of the crema when you make the rosette pattern

- Make a slight rotating motion of wrist (using the hand that is holding the jug) when you make the leaves

- Practice with a larger cup first – that way you get the hang of the swinging action since you have a bigger "canvass" to work with

- Aim to have just the right amount of milk in the cup. Once your pour has already reached the top of the cup it's time to make your strike through.

Chapter 8: Pouring the Tulip Shape

The tulip is another basic piece latte art pattern and it also follows suit with the patterns you did when you made the heart shape as well as with the rosetta shape. This beautiful pattern actually has many variants and you may find other baristas adding other twists and tweaks to their tulips.

Watch how they add their little flourishes so you can incorporate them to your own work. What we'll go over below is the basic tulip. After you get the hang of it, you can make your own tulips with extra flare.

Again, you may want to practice with a larger cup with this one since you will be making several pours. You may end up with an over flowing cup during your practice sessions. You may want to just go up to a third of the way into the cup when you first pour your crema and only then should you start making the tulip shape or pattern.

Note that you will be making several smaller pours with this pattern as you raise the jug up and down a few times. It will take more coordination working with both of your hands when you make this pattern.

So, here's how you do it:

1. As usual you begin by pouring the crema into the shot whilst moving the jug's spout around the cup several times. Do this until the cup is a third of the way full. This gives you a little more room to make several pours to make the tulip pattern.
2. Once you have that stop the milk flow. Next, create a milk stain (sort of circle in the middle of your canvass. After your first pour, cut off the flow of the milk and raise the jug. Don't do this part for too long or else you'll have a huge blob of milk in the middle of the cup. Just one quick dipping pour should be enough. Stop the flow and then raise the jug slightly.
3. Now lower the jug again, pour a second layer from a slightly higher position than the first. As soon as the second pour forming into that circular shape, move the jug to make the second pattern push into the first one you made.
4. Note that the first pattern you made will be compressed as the second shape you made pushes inward.
5. Once the second shape has pushed inward cut the milk flow again while raising the jug slightly.
6. Do the same steps described above pushing the next layer inward on top of the others that you previously formed. Note that the first layers you made will be compressed and made thinner by the newer layers. The newer layers will be fatter or thicker.
7. Once your cup is about full, then raise the jug again and make a strike through linear pour from the top of the tulip pattern all the way to the bottom of the pattern. This will part the image into two parts and thus making your work look like a tulip.

Again, when you practice, it will be easier to start working with a larger cup to avoid spills. Move to a regular shot cup as soon as you get the hang of making multiple pours in a cup without spilling any liquid.

Chapter 9: Pouring the Flower Shape

This will be the final basic shape that we will cover in this book. It's also a free pour method and it will also require several pours as well. Here are the steps to create this pattern.

1. Assuming that you have made your latte shot and have already prepared steamed frothy milk, begin by making the crema layer that will serve as the surface that you will work on.
2. Remember to move the jug around to create a nice and even layer of crema at the surface of the drink. Now you are ready to make the flower pattern.
3. Begin by pouring the milk 2 cm from the edge of the cup. This will serve as the bottom end.
4. When the cup is already half way full, shake the milk just gently while you slowly move from front to back.
5. This will make the pattern move forward as you fill the cup.
6. Shake your wrist a bit moving back and forth to make things easier.
7. When the liquid is almost at the very top of the cup, then stop the flow of the milk.
8. Now make another pour at the top of your image to create a heart shape at the top of the image but make your strike through run from

the heart shape all the way to the bottom of the image that you were making.
9. Notice that making this pattern is like doing a rosetta at the bottom and a small heart shape at the top – sort of a combination of the two patterns that were discussed in the earlier chapters of this book.

Since you are doing two pours, be mindful of the levels of the liquid in your cup to avoid any spills. Note that it will also be easier to make this pattern if you place the cup on top of a table or counter. This will allow you to concentrate on making your pattern rather than getting distracted with balancing the cup in one hand while pouring with the other.

Chapter 10: Etching and Drawing Techniques

Another way to create latte art is by using etching or drawing. You will still be using an espresso, since it is an emulsion that you can use to create your latte art. You will also need to make the crema layer. You can use microfoam for drawing and etching and the good news is that you can also etch without it. Just so you know, the taste of the latte will be affected since the crema forms a huge part of the flavor and taste of latte.

We can say that free pour latte art requires a lot of technical skills. In fact, it may even take a newbie barista several months before he or she can master how to pour the basic patterns perfectly.

In contrast, etching or drawing on your latte will require some true blue artistic skills – as in drawing and painting like skills. Etching in latte art creation is the practice of drawing on coffee. Yes, you read that right, you are literally going to draw on the espresso – well, it is more like drawing on the crema to be exact.

Other than squeezing some chocolate on top of the foam, you will also need to use a toothpick or perhaps a rod (some baristas use the probing tool end of their milk thermometers if they can't find a toothpick immediately). The rod is used to manipulate the crema, the spices, and the other stuff you put on the coffee.

You can make pretty much any image on the coffee from simple lettering to full-fledged sketches of people and things. Some crazy skilled baristas are even able to create full 3D art on their coffee – your creativity is the limit.

What You Need

Here are the basic tools that you will need to etch or draw on your latte:

- Aerated steamed milk (you should know the drill by now)

- Espresso, use fresh pulls if you intend to serve your work to actual people

- Pitchers

- Espresso machine (so you can make your coffee and froth your milk)

- Latte cups (use the 14 ounce ones)

- Thermometer (check the temperature of the milk and the coffee too if you like)

- Syrup (in a container that you can squeeze out), spices, cinnamon, tiny marshmallows, chocolate grounds, and anything that you can use to decorate your coffee.

- Stencils with etched patterns on them

- Skewer or toothpick

General Etching and Instructions

- **Etching:** after you make the crema on top of the espresso, you can etch or draw on the top using a toothpick or perhaps a skewer. The idea is to drag the skewer across the foam to create patterns. The etched image you make will allow the beverage to flow into some parts of the foam on top, which would make the necessary marks so that the design will be clearly visible. You can use this technique to write words on your latte. You can also just drizzle some syrup on top of the foam and then move it around with a toothpick. You can also just write words with the syrup instead.

- **Stencils:** Other than etching words and patterns, you can also use stencils. These are pieces of plastic or wax paper with pattern or design cut outs on them. You can buy them from eBay or from Amazon and they're really cheap. The idea with stencils is simple.

Hold the stencil above the cup (about a centimeter only – try to keep it as close to the froth as much as possible to make the results clear). Pour chocolate, cinnamon, or some other spice or combination of spices on top. Set the stencil aside and now you will see on top of the crema that the powder that you placed has now taken the shape of the cut outs on the stencil.

You can actually make your custom DIY coffee latte stencils. You just need some thin plastic or wax paper (both of which can be bought in any grocery store). You will then print out a pattern that you like using your computer's printer on paper. Just make sure that the size of the print out fits the inside of your coffee cup.

Cut a circle around the pattern the size of your coffee cup. Make the same circular cut matching the size of your cup as well on the plastic or wax paper – add some allowance so you can have something to hold on to.

Stick the pattern on the circle on the plastic or wax paper and then cut out the design on the print out using a cardboard cutter (or some other cutting instrument that is sharp enough).

Smoothen out the cut out on the plastic or wax paper. Hold the cut out on top of your latte and then sprinkle chocolate grounds or your choice of spices for your coffee.

Chocolate Madness: This isn't really an etching technique but an added effect that you can do when you make your drawings or etch work. You can sprinkle some cocoa powder on the espresso before you pour your crema. You will then see some speckles on your latte which is an added highlight to your work. You can then start etching with those accents floating around the foam on top.

Snow Flake

Here's the template for the snow flake pattern on top of crema:

A snow flake is one of the basic patterns you can etch on top of your latte. It doesn't require much effort too. You also don't need any additional stuff like cocoa or choco powder or even syrup to drizzle on it. However, you can use those to add more detail. But here is the basic pattern on how to make it.

The first step is to create the crema on top, you can review the steps on how to make the layer of foam on your latte in the earlier chapter of this book if you like.

Once you have a good crema layer on top begin by making the vertical line at the center. After that make the central "x" pattern crisscrossing the center line you just made. Finally add two small "v" lines to all six ends of the pattern to make your snowflake.

Alternatively, you can cut out the pattern above on a stencil and just sprinkle spices on top.

Clock Template

Here is the template for a clock on top of your latte:

Notice the precision of the lines on this particular piece. You can actually make this by hand but it will require a lot of skill. To make the lines straight, you will need to use a ruler. Place the rule on top of the cup and then glide the syrup container to make the lines of the clock. Now that will require a lot of hard work and really steady hands.

If you want to make your life a lot easier especially if you want the image to be more precise, then you should use a stencil. Cut out the above pattern of a clock on a piece of plastic or wax paper. Sprinkle some cocoa powder or your choice of spice(s) on top and you're done.

Fuel Gauge

Ok, this one is for motor heads and those who drive around a lot:

Again, this will require a lot of precision and talent if you will be doing it by hand. The better and easier option of course is via stencil. Of course, if you want to add some details then you can add some lines on the foam using your choice of syrup.

Floral Pattern

Here is the template for a floral pattern that you can make on your latte. You can actually add whipped cream on top as a finishing touch if you like.

Here's how you make this floral pattern:

1. After making your crema layer, make a small circle at the center. You can use chocolate or some other syrup. If you want to have a little bit of a brownish accent and alternative taste to your drink then use some caramel.
2. After making the first circle at the center, draw another circle around it. Draw several layers of circles around the first few circles that you have made. Make about 5 circles. When you're done, your cup will look like an archery target.
3. Grab a skewer or toothpick (you can also use the stainless steel probe on your milk thermometer if you like). Starting at the center of the circles, drag a line going upwards with your instrument.
4. Now glide from the center going downwards.
5. Next, glide it sideways to the left.
6. After that, glide it sidewards from the center to the left.
7. Now that you're done with the strokes that start from the center, it's time to work on the diagonals. These strokes start from the sides going to the center of the pattern. Notice that you have divided the crema into four quadrants.

8. Draw a diagonal from the edge to the center on the first diagonal (the one on the top left).
9. Now do the diagonal from the edge to the center on the second quadrant (the one on the top right).
10. Repeat the process, but this time do the bottom left.
11. Finally, repeat the same process and this time do the last section, the one on the bottom right.
12. Now you're ready to serve.

Simple Swirl Pattern

This is a simple swirl pattern that you can make quickly without a fuss:

Here's how you can make this design:

1. Sprinkle some cocoa around the sides of the crema.
2. Grab a skewer and spin it around the surface either in a clockwise or counter-clockwise pattern. This will make a swirl pattern on the crema.
3. Finally, sprinkle some more cocoa at the center of the pattern that you have created. If you don't want more cocoa on your latte then you can add some other spice on the top center.
4. You can also add some details like a line of marshmallows on one side of the cup and then some chocolate syrup or caramel syrup lined in a zig zag pattern along the swirl.

The Basic Spread

Now, here is a little technique that you can to your creations to add a little dimension to the image.

Notice that the edges of the pattern are spread to the sides as if they were brush strokes. You will use a spoon or some other implement (perhaps a tiny spatula?) to spread the crema on top.

Alternatively you can add a thin layer of whipped cream on top and then you will spread that into a pattern, like a plant or flower. You will then spread the edges of the image to create a thinning effect.

To add color and contrast, you can sprinkle some cocoa or some other spice that you like on one edge or side of the cup to darken it a bit. And then you will add your whipped cream, followed by the etching work and make the spread effect.

Next, here we have a panda pattern, which you can make using a stencil:

And finally, we have the floral slash swirly pattern again but this time you have a bit of a color contrast in the center.

You will use choco syrup for the lines and to make the slightly darker coloration at the center, sprinkle some cocoa powder at the center circle. And then you can drag a skewer through the pattern to shape the lines accordingly.

Conclusion

Again, thank you for purchasing this book. May the information contained here help you improve your barista skills. The next step is to get your tools ready, buy your supplies, get an espresso machine if you want to (and if you're really serious about this stuff), and start making your beautiful works of art.

Remember that the latte art you make is just icing on the cake. Just as important as your latte art skills is your skill at making wonderful coffee.

Again, to your success,

Ciao!

Printed in Great Britain
by Amazon

37717043R00030